Ancient History for Kids

Civilizations & People

Children's Ancient History Books

Left Brain Kids

Educational Books for Children

ANCIENT CIVILIZATIONS IN THE WORLD

Let's dig into Ancient Civilizations to discover some very interesting facts about the longest and oldest civilization in the world.

ANCIENT CIVILIZATION IN CHINA

The rich culture in China started 4,000 years ago. China is located in East Asia and is considered the biggest country in the world.

There are two major rivers that run across the country, and these are the Yangtze River, and Yellow River.

One of its historical structures, the Great Wall of China, was built during the Quin dynasty but was completed during the Ming dynasty.

The Great Wall of China is also called the "Wan Li Chan Cheng".

Throughout the history of China, 13 dynasties ruled. Yin dynasty was the first, and the Qing dynasty was the last.

Ancient China had the longest running empire in the world. In 221 BC, China had its first emperor, QuinShihuang.

Quin planned and began to build the Great Wall of China. He also united all of China under one rule.

The last Chinese Emperor, Puyi, became a ruler when he was just 3 years old. Puyi succeeded his uncle Guangxu when he died on November 1908. Puyi started his reign on 1908 amd ended 1912.

In ancient China, the dragon symbolized the emperor for power, luck, and strength. Many years ago, China was under the feudal system of government.

In this system, there were landlords who owned the lands, while peasant farmers worked for them.

In the next years, the empire was run by officials of the civil service. These officials oversaw the the collection of taxes and the enforcement of laws.

Chinese men needed to pass a series of examinations before they could become officials.

The Chinese scholars, who were officials at that time, were the most respected class of people in Ancient China.

Next to them were the peasants because they produced the food for the entire country. In ancient China, arts and culture, including religion, were often interrelated.

The three main philosophies or religions in China were Buddhism, Confucianism, and Taoism.

These philosophies, called "the three ways", created a very huge impact among the Chinese people's way of living, and even in their expression of art.

The focus of Chinese art is "the three perfections";

- ⚜ calligraphy
- ⚜ painting
- ⚜ poetry.

When the printing press was invented, the most known printed booklet was the book of Buddhist prayers and sayings.

The "Art of War", written by military strategist Sun Tzu, was the most famous book printed and it talked about battle strategies.

Although the book was printed more than 2500 years ago, it has been quoted often, even to this day.

When it comes to food traditions, the Chinese people have always used chopsticks to eat.

Moreover, they were the first group of people who drank tea, primarily for medical purposes.

ANCIENT CIVILIZATION OF EGYPT

Egyptian Civilization is considered to be the "mother of all civilizations" in the world history. Ancient Egypt was gifted with the Nile River, which gave birth to the civilization.

The Nile River, flows water from the middle of Africa down to the Mediterranean Sea, and nourished the success of the pharaonic kingdom.

The long and narrow river became a magnet of life, which attracted people, plants and animals to dwell on the banks.

During the pre-dynasty, there were nomadic hunters that lived among the valley. They began to plant crops to supply their own food.

The people considered the Nile River a gift from the gods; annual flooding in the river made a rich deposit on the land, and it became ideal for planting wheat and flax among other crops.

The first project done by the community was to build the irrigation canals which were needed for their agriculture.

EGYPTIAN BELIEFS

The Egyptians worshipped the sun as their main deity, and they believed that the passing through of the sun in the sky represented an eternal life cycle; of birth and death, and even rebirth.

They perceived the pharaohs as gods, who were divine representatives in the Earth, and would ensure continuity of life, through rituals.

They also believed after death, they would become immortal, and would join their gods in afterlife. Moreover, Egyptians believed their bodies and souls were very important in their existence on Earth and also after they died.

The funerary practices, like mummification and the burial in the tombs, were created to usher their deceased bodies in their journey to their second life.

Tombs had to be filled with their necessities in life; food, domestic wares and tools and even treasures, to make sure their souls would return to their deceased bodies.

Egyptians tombs were the Egyptian pyramids, like the Pyramids of Giza, and these structures have became the first wonders of the world.

Did you have fun reading
about Ancient Civilizations?

Share this book with
your friends!

www.ingramcontent.com/pod-product-compliance
Lightning Source LLC
Chambersburg PA
CBHW081233020426
42331CB00012B/3153